PINOCCHIO

Comprehension Guide
by Deb Chapin and
Laurie Detweiler

Designed by
Ned Bustard

www.VeritasPress.com
(800) 922-5082

Copyright ©2003 Veritas Press
www.VeritasPress.com
(800) 922-5082
ISBN 1-932168-07-9

Printed in the United States of America.

PINOCCHIO
How to Use this Guide

This guide is intended to help you study, understand, and enjoy *Pinocchio.* You might ask if a guide is really necessary to read a book. Is the student not just working to improve reading skills while being taught to enjoy reading a book? Certainly, it is the case that the more a child reads, the more he should improve his skills, but quantity is not the only issue. Once a child has received adequate phonetic training hc should learn how to read a book. Most educators using this guide will be teaching children in the grammar stage, generally understood to be during the elementary years in a classical education. (For a thorough understanding of classical Christian education, we recommend reading *Recovering the Lost Tools of Learning* or *The Case for Classical Christian Education,* both by Douglas Wilson.) The basic goals of reading in the grammar stage are as follows:

The student should be able to:
1. Fluently read a given selection orally.
2. Show an increased desire for reading.
3. Show comprehension on a literal and inferential level.
4. Demonstrate an increased vocabulary.
5. Identify basic Biblical values in the literature being read.
6. Identify various styles (myths, poems, fantasy, fiction, nonfiction, etc.)

Answers to the questions are found in the back of the guide. The students' answers should be in complete sentences, and they should restate the question in their answer.

Example:

Question: Why did Pinocchio fall as he tried to open the door for Geppetto?

Answer: Pinocchio fell because his feet had burned off.

Such writing practice trains the student to answer thoroughly, completely, and with proper grammar. Another reason is to encourage integration. We want students to understand that how they write something is as important as what they write.

The question of grading is one that always arises. Unless otherwise indicated you should assume that each question is worth five points.

PINOCCHIO
Chapter 1

1. The author of the book Pinocchio was _____.

2 The book Pinocchio was illustrated by _____.

3. The translator of the book Pinocchio was _____.

4. Why was Master Antonio called Master Cherry?

_____

_____

_____

_____

5. What happened when Master Cherry first started to use the axe on the piece of wood?

_____

_____

_____

6. What did Master Cherry do to encourage himself when he was frightened?

_____

_____

_____

_____

_____

PINOCCHIO
Chapter 1, Project

*Imagine that a piece of wood began to speak
to you. What would the wood say?*

_____

_____

_____

_____

_____

_____

_____

_____

_____

_____

_____

_____

_____

_____

_____

_____

_____

*Write a play to be performed by two students—one being a piece of wood and the other
being Master Cherry.*

PINOCCHIO
Chapter 2

1. Why was the nickname Polendina given to Geppetto?

   Geppetto was nicknamed Polendina becouse he had a yellow wig.

2. How did Geppetto act when people called him Polendina?

   Geppetto

3. Describe what happened when Master Cherry gave Geppetto the piece of wood.

   Master Cherry went to go and give Geppetto the piece of wood and it sliped out of his hands and hit Geppetto in the shin.

Pinocchio
Chapter 2, Project—Marionette

Pinocchio began as a block of wood and most of the materials in this project began in the same form. The difference is, there will be much less whittling on this doll.

Materials

4 4.5 oz. soap bar boxes

1 Tissue box (150 2-ply—4.25" x 8.75" x 3.75")

String or yarn

8 toilet paper rolls

Newspaper

Masking Tape

Wallpaper

Black construction paper

Permanent Markers (black and red)

Pencil

Hanger

Instructions

Cut sheets of newspaper into strips. Crumple 4 or 5 strips into a ball. Wind the other strips around the ball. Apply tape from time to time to keep it from coming undone. When the ball is the size of your fist, tape a two foot length of string onto it, with 4" hanging off one side. Continue wrapping until the ball is the size for Pinocchio's head in proportion to the body, and push the pointed end of the pencil into the head to the length of honesty desired. Finish it off by winding masking tape around the pencil to form the nose and around the head to cover the newspaper. Using permanent markers, draw eyes, hair, mouth, and rosy cheeks. Attach his head by securely taping the 4" length of yarn onto the center of the end of the tissue box. Wrap each of the four toilet rolls and the tissue box on all sides in wallpaper, which represents his clothing. Cover the four toilet rolls and two soap boxes in masking tape for his lower arms, hands, and lower legs. Wrap two soap boxes in black construction paper for his shoes. Run string through the toilet rolls to form the limbs, taping them down at each joint inside the rolls. For each limb, tape off one end of the string at the hand or foot and the other end at the appropriate place on the torso. Leave enough slack so the limbs will be able to move freely. Attach the puppet to the hanger with another string secured to the top of the torso, behind Pinocchio's head. Run a string from each elbow and knee, tying the ends to the hanger as shown. Manipulate the hanger to make your marionette "come to life."

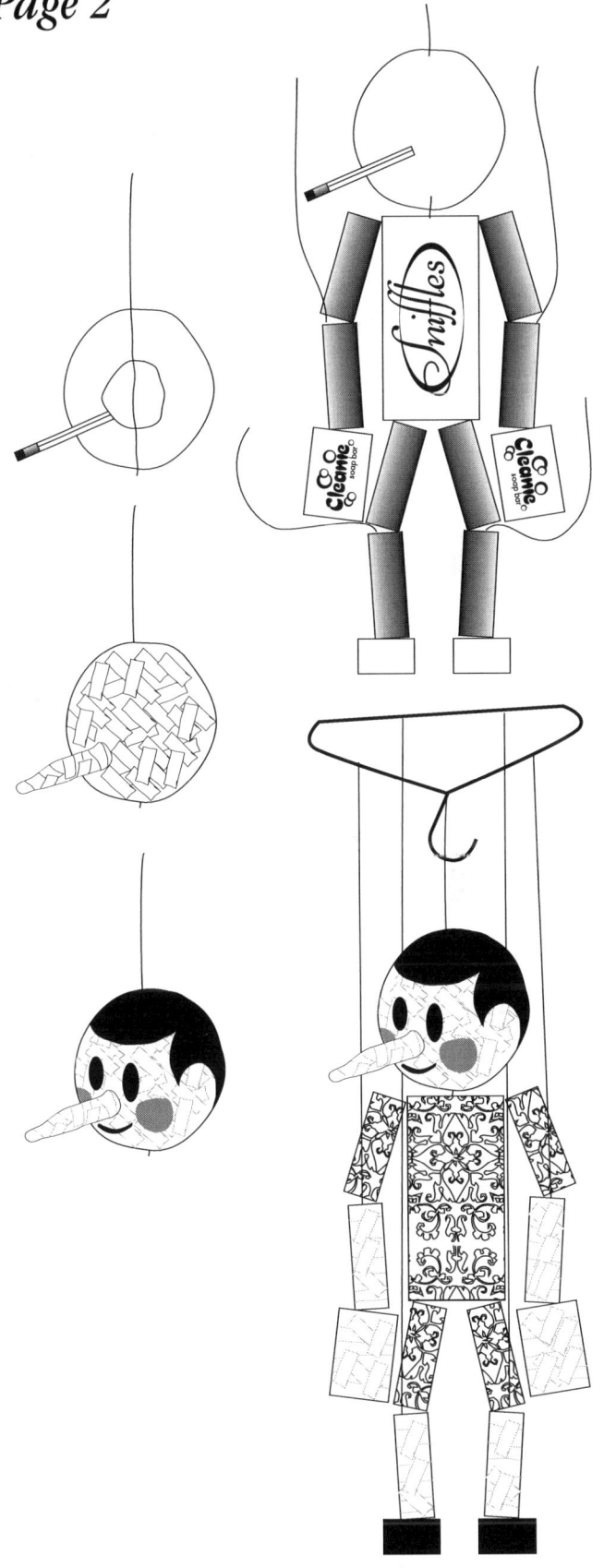

PINOCCHIO
Chapter 3

1. Describe where Geppetto lived.

_____

_____

2. What did Geppetto do as soon as he got home?

_____

_____

3. What happened when Geppetto carved the nose on the puppet?

_____

_____

4. What happened right after Geppetto carved the hands?

_____

_____

5. What did Geppetto decide to name the puppet?

_____

_____

6. Why was Geppetto taken to prison?

_____

_____

Pinocchio
Chapter 3, Project

Draw an illustration (picture) of a scene described in the chapter.

PINOCCHIO
Chapter 4

1. What did Pinocchio do as Geppetto was being taken to prison?

_____

_____

2. Whom did Pinocchio meet in the house?

_____

_____

3. What truth does the cricket tell Pinocchio?

_____

_____

4. Why did Pinocchio tell the cricket he was going to run away?

_____

_____

5. What was the only trade in the world that took Pinocchio's fancy?

_____

_____

6. What did Pinocchio do to the cricket?

_____

_____

Pinocchio
Chapter 4, Project

Write a paragraph about why Pinocchio killed the messenger.

_____

_____

_____

_____

_____

_____

_____

_____

_____

_____

_____

_____

_____

_____

PINOCCHIO
Chapters 5 and 6

1. Describe what happened
   in these chapters as
   Pinocchio realized
   how hungry he was and
   what happened as he went in
   search of food.

PINOCCHIO
Chapters 5 and 6, Project—Italian Omelette

Poor Pinocchio didn't get to make an omelette, but by following the recipe below, you can cook a delicious Italian omelette for yourself.

Ingredients

3 1/2 oz cooked pasta

2 eggs

2 tablespoons grated Parmesan cheese

8 tablespoons olive oil

salt

chopped tomatoes

Directions

Beat the eggs in a bowl, dust with cheese and season with salt. Throw in the pasta and stir. Meanwhile heat a well-oiled frying pan and pour in the mixture, stirring with a wooden spoon. Let the eggs set over reduced heat. Sprinkle the tomatoes on half the omelette. Fold over the omelette. Cook well the other side.

PINOCCHIO
Chapter 7

1. Why did Pinocchio fall as he tried to open the door for Geppetto?

   _____

   _____

2. What did Geppetto do when he saw Pinocchio's burnt feet?

   _____

   _____

3. What did Geppetto give Pinocchio to eat?

   _____

   _____

4. What did Geppetto mean when he said,

   ". . . You should not be so refined and fastidious about

   your food. My dear boy, we never know what

   might happen to us . . . ?"

   _____

   _____

   _____

   _____

   _____

   _____

Pinocchio
Chapter 7, Project—Bookmark

On the bookmark below, make a list of some foods that you do not like that you could learn to like. Color and cut out to use as you continue reading through this book.

PINOCCHIO
Chapter 8

1. How long did it take Geppetto to make two feet for Pinocchio?

_____

_____

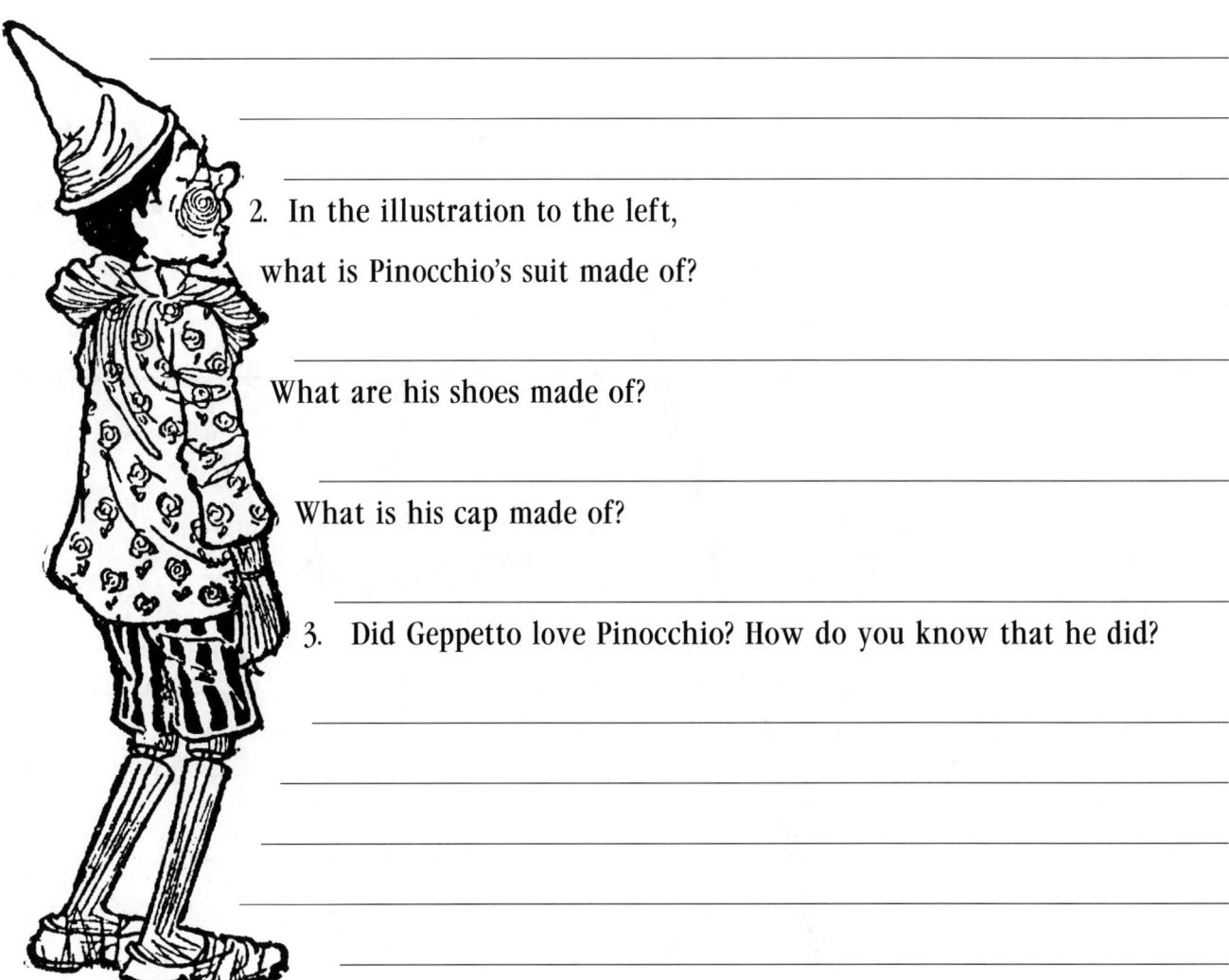

2. In the illustration to the left,

   what is Pinocchio's suit made of?

_____

What are his shoes made of?

_____

What is his cap made of?

_____

3. Did Geppetto love Pinocchio? How do you know that he did?

_____

_____

_____

_____

PINOCCHIO
Chapter 8, Project—Primer

On the pages provided make a primer for Pinocchio. Draw a large capital letter on each page and a picture of an object that starts with that letter. Color. Then assemble into a book by cutting along dashed lines and folding on dotted lines.

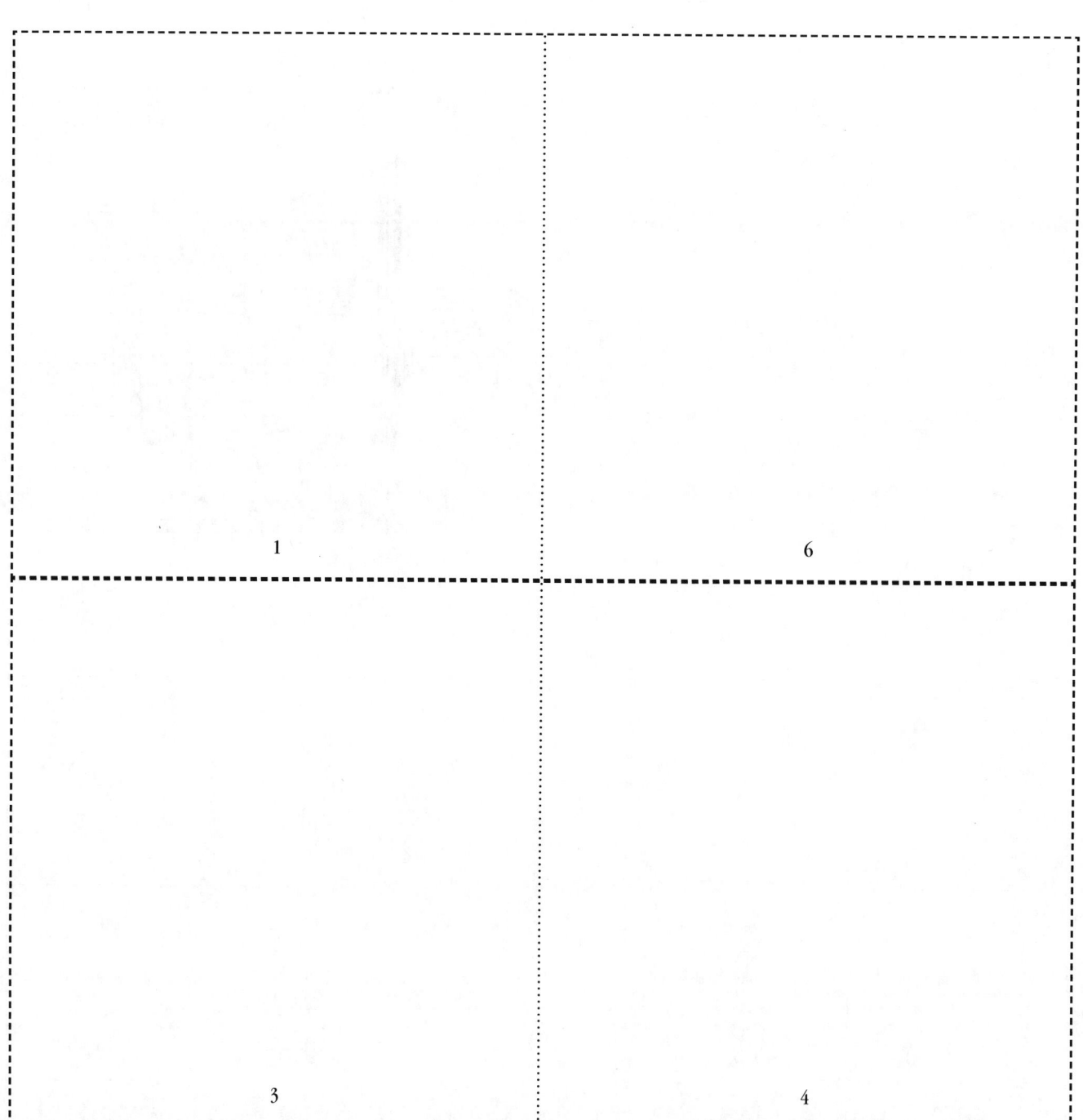

PINOCCHIO
Chapter 9

Vocabulary:

Primer:

_____

_____

Twopence:

_____

_____

1. Describe the castles in the air that Pinocchio imagined and planned on the way to school?

_____

_____

_____

2. Why did the boy not want to buy Pinocchio's clothes?

_____

_____

3. How would you have felt if you sold the primer for twopence that had cost Geppetto his coat?

_____

_____

_____

_____

PINOCCHIO
Chapter 9, Project—Thank You Note

How do your parents sacrifice for you?
Write them a letter listing three things
that you are thankful for.

PINOCCHIO
Chapter 10-13

1. Which puppet recognized Pinocchio in the audience.

   _____

   _____

   _____

2. What did the Showman look like?

   _____

   _____

   _____

3. In chapter 11 we learn the Showman's
   name. What was his name?

   _____

4. What was it that caused Fire-eater to sneeze?

   _____

   _____

5. What did the Showman give to Pinocchio to give to Geppetto?

   _____

   _____

6. In chapter 12, what were the words of the song that the white blackbird sang?

   _____

   _____

7. Fill in the blank: "_____ children never do any good in this world."

8. How did the fox and the cat say that Pinocchio could make his five gold pieces into two thousand in one day?

_____

_____

_____

9. Do you think it was wise of Pinocchio to go with the cat and the fox?

_____

_____

_____

10. What happened at the Red Crab Inn?

_____

_____

_____

_____

11. What advice did the ghost of the talking cricket give to Pinocchio?

_____

_____

_____

_____

_____

PINOCCHIO
Chapter 10-13, Project

Write an opinion paragraph: Why do you think Pinocchio did not listen to the advice given by the ghost of the talking cricket?

PINOCCHIO
Chapter 14–16

1. What did Pinocchio do with his gold pieces when he saw the assassins?

_____

_____

_____

2. What did the assassins do when Pinocchio climbed a very tall pine-tree and sat on the highest branch?

_____

_____

_____

3. Describe the child that opened the window of the little house.

_____

_____

_____

_____

4. Why did the assassins hang Pinocchio?

_____

_____

_____

5. Who saved Pinocchio?

_____

_____

_____

6. Who were the three doctors that were sent for?

_____

_____

_____

7. What happened when the talking cricket said, "That puppet is a disobedient son, who will make his poor old father die of a broken heart!"?

_____

_____

_____

_____

_____

PINOCCHIO
Chapters 14–16, Project

List two incidents from the chapters that document that Pinocchio is changing for the better.

_____

_____

_____

_____

_____

_____

_____

_____

_____

_____

_____

PINOCCHIO
Chapter 17

1. List some reasons why Pinocchio said he was
   unable to drink the bitter medicine
   that the fairy gave to him.

   _____

   _____

   _____

   _____

2. What made him change his mind and decide to drink
   the medicine?

   _____

   _____

   _____

3. What does it mean to "fear the medicine more than the sickness?"

   _____

   _____

4. Describe what happened when Pinocchio told a lie.

   _____

   _____

   _____

   _____

PINOCCHIO
Chapter 18

1. Why did the fairy let the puppet scream and cry a good half-hour because of his long nose, which he could not get through the door?

_____

_____

_____

_____

2. Draw a picture of what you think Pinocchio's nose looked like.

PINOCCHIO
Chapter 18, Project

Make a list of some foolish things that children about your age can do.

PINOCCHIO
Chapter 19

1. In what way was Pinocchio a simpleton?

   _____

   _____

   _____

2. Who placed Pinocchio in prison?

   _____

   _____

   _____

3. What kind of people received their freedom during the great public rejoicing?

   _____

   _____

   _____

PINOCCHIO
Chapter 19, Project

Look up justice in the dictionary. Then in the space provided below, write about how Pinocchio's treatment by the old gorilla judge seems unjust.

Justice:

PINOCCHIO
Chapter 20

1. At the beginning of chapter 20 Pinocchio recognized that he deserved some of the dreadful things that had happened to him. In what way was he an obstinate mule?

   _____

   _____

   _____

2. What lesson did he learn?

   _____

   _____

   _____

   _____

3. What did he want to do differently?

   _____

   _____

   _____

PINOCCHIO
Chapter 21

1. Do you think that Pinocchio should have picked grapes?

    _____

    _____

    _____

2. What did the firefly tell him about taking what is not yours?

    _____

    _____

    _____

    _____

3. What do you think Pinocchio meant when he said at the end of chapter 21, "Oh, if I could only be born again!"?

    _____

    _____

    _____

    _____

PINOCCHIO
Chapter 22

1. What kind of watchdog was Melampo?

   _____

   _____

2. What did Pinocchio do when the four polecats went inside the poultry yard?

   _____

   _____

3. Why didn't Pinocchio tell the peasant about the agreement between the dog and the polecats?

   _____

   _____

4. How did the peasant show Pinocchio how grateful he was?

   _____

   _____

   _____

PINOCCHIO
Chapter 23

1. When Pinocchio reached the field where the little white house had once stood, what did he find?

    _____

    _____

    _____

2. What was Pinocchio's response to the death of the beautiful child with blue hair?

    _____

    _____

    _____

3. What did the large pigeon tell Pinocchio?

    _____

    _____

    _____

4. Why did Pinocchio jump into the sea?

    _____

    _____

    _____

    _____

    _____

    _____

    _____

PINOCCHIO
Chapter 24

1. After Pinocchio is on the island, whom does he first meet?

   _____

   _____

2. How does Pinocchio describe his father and himself to the fish?

   _____

   _____

   _____

3. Why did lazy Pinocchio not like the Busy Bee town?

   _____

   _____

   _____

4. What had Pinocchio's father told him about begging
   for food that made him ashamed to beg?

   _____

   _____

   _____

5. Who finally gave Pinocchio food?

   _____

   _____

   _____

PINOCCHIO
Chapter 25

1. The fairy told Pinocchio that he could become a man if he were a good boy. List the four things that good boys are:

   1. _____

   _____

   2. _____

   _____

   3. _____

   _____

   4. _____

   _____

2. Why did the fairy forgive Pinocchio?

   _____

   _____

   _____

   _____

   _____

3. According to the fairy, what happens to people who don't like work?

   _____

   _____

   _____

   _____

   _____

PINOCCHIO
Chapter 25, Project—Word Search

```
C   A   S   D   F   G   H   J   K   L
M   H   L   O   V   E   P   O   I   U
O   M   I   D   L   E   N   E   S   S
T   F   U   L   Y   T   R   E   W   Q
H   A   M   L   D   Z   X   V   B   N
E   I   Q   W   E   H   C   G   H   J
R   R   T   Y   U   I   O   P   L   K
S   Y   A   D   F   B   X   O   K   L
X   D   E   S   E   R   V   E   D   T
Q   W   E   R   T   Y   U   I   O   Z
```

1. The little woman turned out to be the blue-haired _____.

2. Pinocchio recognized the blue-haired fairy by his _____ for her.

3. The blue-haired fairy said she was old enough to be Pinocchio's _____.

4. Pinocchio learned he could become a boy only if he _____ it.

5. _____ is a dreadful disease,

    of which one should be cured

    immediately in _____;

    if not, one never gets it.

I WILL BE GOOD

PINOCCHIO
Chapter 26

Pinocchio is now going to school. The schoolmaster praised him for he found him attentive, studious and intelligent. But he had one fault. Write a descriptive paragraph about this fault and what it caused him to do.

PINOCCHIO
Chapter 27

1. Why had the boys deceived Pinocchio?

   _____

   _____

2. Describe the fight between Pinocchio and the boys.

   _____

   _____

   _____

3. What happened to Eugene?

   _____

   _____

   _____

4. Why did the carabineers/police-
   men take Pinocchio away?

   _____

   _____

   _____

   _____

5. When Pinocchio's cap fell off,
   what did he decide to do?

   _____

   _____

   _____

   _____

PINOCCHIO
Chapter 28

1. What was the name of the dog [dreadful beast] that was sent to chase Pinocchio?

    _____

    _____

2. What did Pinocchio do that saved the dog's life?

    _____

    _____

    _____

3. Describe the fisherman that caught Pinocchio in a net.

    _____

    _____

    _____

    _____

4. What kind of fish did the fisherman think Pinocchio was?

    _____

    _____

    _____

5. What did the fisherman do with Pinocchio?

    _____

    _____

    _____

PINOCCHIO
Chapter 28, Project

Describe the following: [You may use a dictionary or encyclopedia]

Sardines

_____

_____

Crabs

_____

_____

Anchovies

_____

_____

Mullet

_____

_____

Whiting

_____

_____

PINOCCHIO
Chapter 29

1. Who saved Pinocchio from the fisherman's frying pan?

   _____

   _____

   _____

2. Why did he save him?

   _____

   _____

   _____

3. How did Pinocchio get his foot stuck in the door?

   _____

   _____

   _____

4. The fairy told Pinocchio she would pardon him once more. What did she tell him would happen tomorrow?

   _____

   _____

   _____

   _____

Pinocchio
Chapter 29, Project—Celebration Breakfast

In Chapter twenty-nine the fairy announced that Pinocchio's wish would be granted and that he would cease to be a puppet and become a real boy. In order to celebrate, all Pinocchio's classmates were invited to the fairy's house for a grand breakfast to mark this important event. The fairy prepared two hundred cups of coffee with cream and four hundred bread rolls, buttered on both sides. *Make a grand breakfast to celebrate, including coffee with cream and bread rolls buttered on both sides. Use the invitation below.*

You are cordially invited to a Celebration Breakfast for Pinocchio consisting of coffee with cream and bread rolls buttered on both sides

DATE: _____

TIME: _____

RSVP By: _____

PINOCCHIO
Chapter 30

1. The fairy told Pinocchio "Children who do not follow the advice of those who are wiser than they are, always come to grief." In your own words explain what that means.

   _____

   _____

   _____

2. What was to be served at the grand breakfast?

   _____

   _____

   _____

3. What kind of boy was Lampwick?

   _____

   _____

   _____

4. How did Lampwick describe Playland?

   _____

   _____

   _____

   _____

PINOCCHIO
Chapter 31

1. Describe the twelve pairs of donkeys that drew the coach?

    _____

    _____

    _____

    _____

2. Do you think that the driver of the coach was nice or not nice? Explain your answer.

    _____

    _____

    _____

3. After Pinocchio mounted the donkey and the donkeys galloped and the coach rolled over the paving stones, what did a low voice say?

    _____

    _____

    _____

PINOCCHIO
Chapter 31, Project—Playland

Draw a picture of what you think Playland may have looked like. Then write what you think the perfect playland would be like.

```
MAP OF PLAYLAND
```

_____

_____

_____

_____

_____

_____

_____

PINOCCHIO
Chapter 32

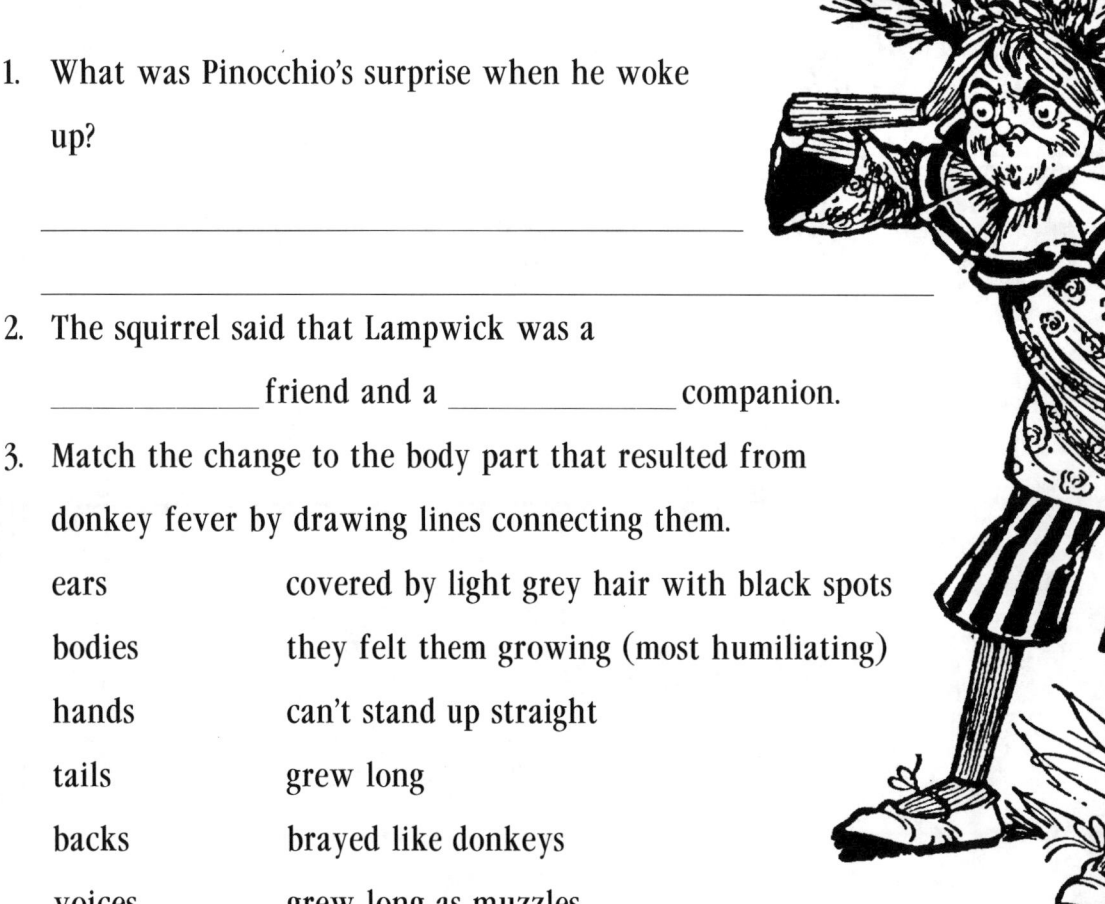

1. What was Pinocchio's surprise when he woke up?

   _____

   _____

2. The squirrel said that Lampwick was a

   _____ friend and a _____ companion.

3. Match the change to the body part that resulted from donkey fever by drawing lines connecting them.

   ears   covered by light grey hair with black spots

   bodies   they felt them growing (most humiliating)

   hands   can't stand up straight

   tails   grew long

   backs   brayed like donkeys

   voices   grew long as muzzles

   faces   became hoofs

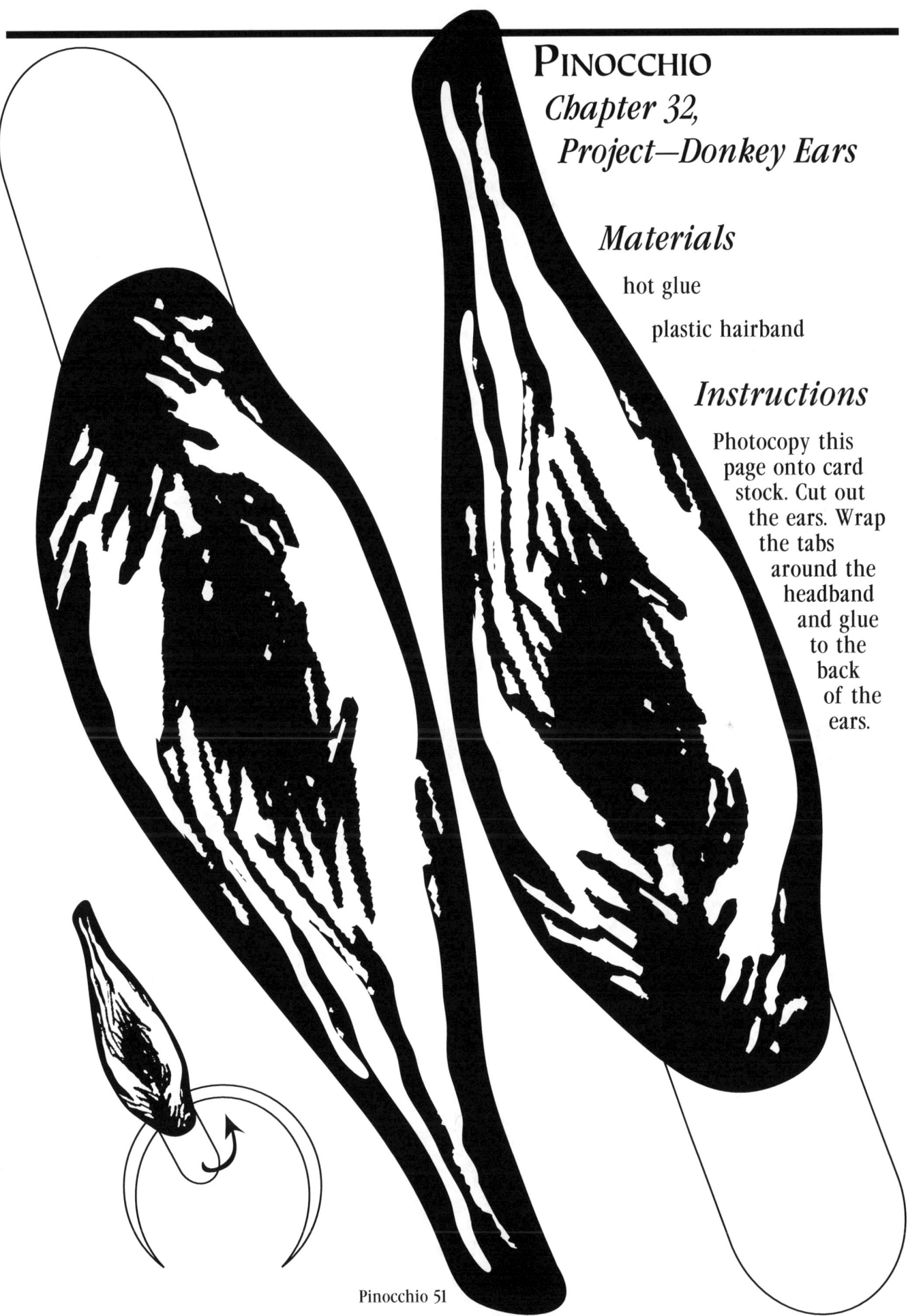

PINOCCHIO
Chapter 32,
Project—Donkey Ears

Materials

hot glue

plastic hairband

Instructions

Photocopy this page onto card stock. Cut out the ears. Wrap the tabs around the headband and glue to the back of the ears.

PINOCCHIO
Chapter 33

1. What was the cruel little man doing to children?

    _____

    _____

2. Which did Pinocchio like better, hay or straw?

    _____

    _____

3. Draw a picture of Pinocchio the donkey performing

Pinocchio

Chapter 33, Project—Circus Poster

In chapter
thirty-three
Pinocchio
is sold to a
manager of
a show to
perform.
*In the frame
to the right,
draw a poster
they might
have put up
in town.*

Pinocchio
Chapter 34

1. When Pinocchio's purchaser pulled the rope up out of the water, what was on the other end of it?

   _____

   _____

2. How did Pinocchio get the man to untie him?

   _____

   _____

   _____

   _____

3. What story did Pinocchio tell the man who purchased him?

   _____

   _____

   _____

   _____

4. What happened to Pinocchio when he tried to escape?

   _____

   _____

   _____

PINOCCHIO
Chapter 34, Project

Pinocchio isn't the only famous person swallowed by a fish. Write the story in your own words about the man who long ago was swallowed up by a huge fish and lived to tell the tale.

_____

_____

_____

_____

_____

_____

_____

_____

_____

_____

_____

_____

_____

PINOCCHIO
Chapter 35

1. Draw a picture
   of what Pinocchio
   saw as he walked
   through the body
   of the shark
   (or dogfish).

2. What did
   Pinocchio tell his father that they must do?

PINOCCHIO
Chapter 35, Project—Cartoon

Draw a cartoon of the escape.

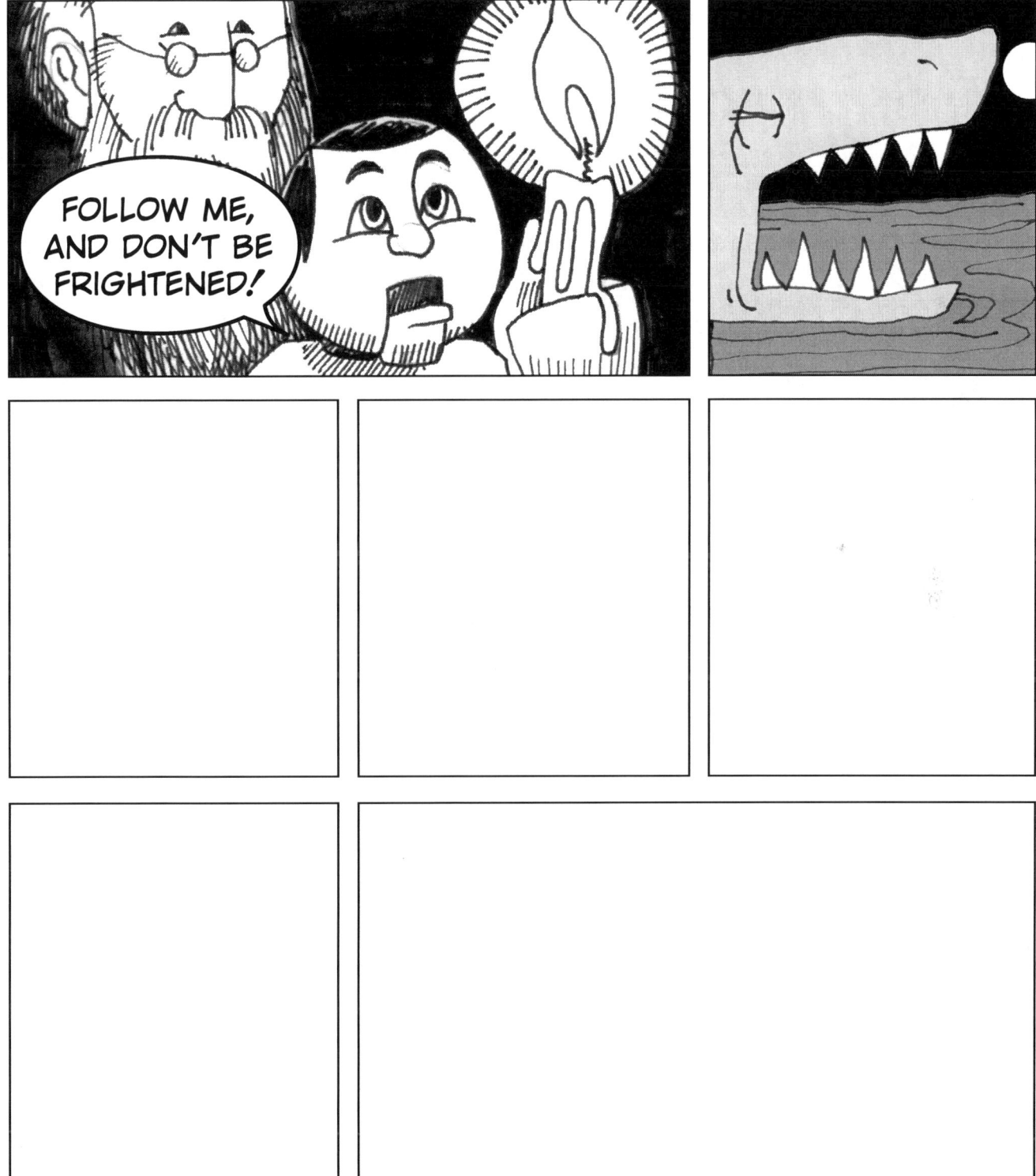

PINOCCHIO
Chapter 36

1. Who saved Pinocchio and Geppetto?

_____

2. What did Pinocchio do to thank the tunny?

_____

_____

3. What did the cricket do when Pinocchio and Geppetto came to his house?

_____

_____

4. Where did Pinocchio find Candlewick?

_____

_____

5. What did Pinocchio try to do to save the ill fairy?

_____

_____

6. Why was the fairy willing to turn Pinocchio into a boy?

_____

_____

7. What did Geppetto say was the reason for the change in Pinocchio?

_____

_____

_____

_____

PINOCCHIO
Answers

CHAPTER 1
1. Carlo Collodi
2. Gioia Fiammenghi
3. E. Harden
4. He was called Master Cherry because the tip of his nose was red and shiny.
5. it started talking
6. He started to sing to himself.

CHAPTER 2
1. The wig was about the color of polendina (a pudding made of Indian corn)
2. He turned red as a turkey and became very angry.
3. The piece of wood gave a shake, wriggled violently out of his hands and hit Geppetto in the shins.

CHAPTER 3
1. Geppetto live in a ground floor little room with simple furniture of an old chair, tottering bed and a broken-down table and an artificial fire place.
2. He took his tools and began to make the puppet.
3. The nose began to grow.
4. His wig was snatched from his head.
5. Pinocchio
6. Because people blamed Geppetto for Pinocchio's behavior

CHAPTER 4
1. That rascal Pinocchio ran home as quickly as possible.
2. The talking cricket
3. Woe to those boys who revolt against their parents, and run away from home. They will never do any good in this world and sooner or later they will repent bitterly.
4. He would be sent to school.
5. To eat, drink, sleep and amuse myself and to lead a vagabond life from morning to night.
6. He threw a mallet at the cricket which flattened him against the wall.

CHAPTER 5 AND 6
Hungry Pinoccho hunts for an egg so he can make an omelette, but when he breaks the shell a little chicken flies out and away. A kettle of water is poured down on this head, and he goes to Geppetto's to warm himself by the fire. But when he wakes up in the morning his feet have burned off.

CHAPTER 7
1. He fell because his feet had burned off.
2. He took him in his arms, kissed, caressed and spoke kindly to him.
3. He gave him the pears that Geppetto had bought for himself.
4. From childhood we should eat all kinds of food and like it because one does not know what one may have to eat in the future.

CHAPTER 8
1. Less than an hour
2. paper, bark, bread
3. Yes, he loved him, because he sold his coat so that Pinocchio could have a primer.

CHAPTER 9
Primer: an introductory textbook for teaching children to read
Twopence: the sum of two pence, a thing of little value.
1. He imagined that he would learn to read in one day, and the next day write and the next day learn all his figures (numbers). Then earn lots of money to buy his father a gold and silver coat with diamond buttons. Each imagination was more beautiful than the other.
2. Because rain would make the paper wet and not come off, the shoes were only good for lighting a fire and the mice may eat the bread cap right off his head.

PINOCCHIO
Answers

3. Answers may vary.

CHAPTER 10-13
1. Harlequin recognized him.
2. He was very tall, ugly, with a long black ink beard, mouth big as an oven, his eyes like two burning red lanterns, and he cracked a great whip.
3. Fire-eater
4. Fire-eater sneezed when he pitied someone
5. Five gold pieces
6. Pinocchio, don't listen to the advice of evil companions. If you do, you'll regret it.
7. disobedient
8. By putting the gold pieces into a hole in the Field of Miracles and covering and watering them. The next day you will find a tree laden with gold pieces.
9. No.
10. The cat and fox ordered much food and two nice rooms and left poor Pinocchio to pay for it all.
11. Go back home and carry the four gold pieces you have left to your poor father, who is weeping and longing for you.

CHAPTER 14-16
1. He put them in his mouth under his tongue.
2. They tried to climb after him but slipped and fell, so they set fire to the tree.
3. Her hair was blue, and her face as white as wax; her eyes were closed and her hands were crossed on her breast.
4. Because he would not open his mouth
5. The beautiful blue-haired child
6. They were a crow, an owl and a talking cricket.
7. Pinocchio started crying.

CHAPTER 17
1. If it's bitter I won't drink it. I don't like anything bitter. That pillow on my feet annoys me. The door bothers me; it's half open.
2. Four black rabbits who said he was going to die.
3. When one thinks it is better to be sick than to take the medicine.
4. His nose became two inches longer.

CHAPTER 18
1. She did this to teach him a good lesson, and to correct him of the very bad habit of lying.

CHAPTER 19
1. He was silly enough to believe all the nonsense he heard
2. An old gorilla judge
3. Every rascal received his freedom.

CHAPTER 20
1. "I always want my own way, and never listen to those who love me, and who have a thousand times more sense than I have."
2. "I have learned the lesson that disobedient children never prosper, and never gain anything."
3. He wanted to be good, loving and grateful.

CHAPTER 21
1. Answers may vary.
2. Hunger is not a good excuse for taking what is not yours.
3. He was sorry for all of the wrong things that he had done, and he wanted to have a clean record and start again.

CHAPTER 22
1. A dishonest one who helped people steal from the farmer
2. Pinocchio shut the door on them.
3. He thought it would be no good to accuse the dead.
4. He gave him back his freedom.

CHAPTER 23
1. A little piece of white marble engraved with: Here lies the blue-haired child who died of sorrow on being deserted by her little brother Pinocchio.
2. He wept and wailed and moaned all night long.
3. That Geppetto was crossing the ocean to search for Pinocchio
4. to save his father

PINOCCHIO
Answers

CHAPTER 24
1. A big fish
2. He is the best father in the world; and I am very likely the worst son.
3. Because he would have to work to get food in this town
4. Only the aged and the crippled have a right to beg . . . it is everyone else's duty to work
5. The dear fairy

CHAPTER 25
1. 1. good boys are obedient
   2. good boys like to work and study
   3. good boys always tell the truth
   4. good boys like to go to school
2. The fairy forgave him because he was really sorry.
3. They generally end in a hospital, or in a prison.

Project
1. fairy
2. love
3. mother
4. deserved
5. Idleness, childhood

CHAPTER 26
Pinnocchio's one fault was that he made too many friends. Some of these friends were good-for-nothings and unwilling to study. They made him lose his love for books and led him into great trouble. He skipped school, went to the beach where terrors and dreadful disasters were awaiting him.

CHAPTER 27
1. When Pinocchio studied so hard it made the boys look small in the master's eyes.
2. Pinocchio insulted the boys by calling them Coo-coo. The boys shouted, hit, and threw books. The boys threw one of Pinocchio's books, and it hit a boy named Eugene. When Eugene fell, the boys ran away.
3. He cried "Oh, Mamma, help me! I am dying!" And fell his full length on the sand.
4. Since Eugene was injured with Pinocchio's book, they blamed him for the injury.
5. Pinocchio decided to run towards the sea to get away.

CHAPTER 28
1. Alidoro
2. He pulled him by the tail to the safety of the beach.
3. He was so ugly he looked like a sea monster. Leaves grew out of his hands, a long green beard, looking like a huge green lizard, standing on his hind legs.
4. A crab
5. Rolled him in flour.

Project
Sardines: the young of the plichard when a suitable size to preserve for food.
Crabs: any of numerous marine or land crustaceans, distinguished by their short, broad, and unusually flattened carapace.
Anchovies: any of a number of small herring-like fishes.
Mullet: any of a family of valuable food fishes, the gray mullets, occurring in streams and most seas.
Whiting: a common European food fish of the cod family.

CHAPTER 29
1. Alidoro the dog
2. A good turn deserves another.
3. He kicked the door with rage.
4. Tomorrow he would become a real boy.

CHAPTER 30
1. Foolish actions lead to painful consequences.
2. Rolls buttered on both sides to be dipped in coffee and milk
3. The laziest and most mischievous boy in the school
4. The most beautiful country in the world—a real dreamland. No schools, no masters, and no books, no one ever studies, six Saturdays in every week and no Sundays.

CHAPTER 31
1. All the same size, different colors wearing men's boots of white leather.
2. Opinion: mean. He pretended to be kind and sweet but he bit off half of the kicking donkey's right ear.
3. "You poor fool! You decided to do as you please, but you'll be sorry for it!"

PINOCCHIO
Answers

CHAPTER 32
1. He noticed that his ears had grown several inches.
2. The squirrel said that Lampwick was a false friend and a bad companion.
3. ears—grew long
   bodies—can't stand up straight
   hands—became hoofs
   tails—they felt them growing (most humiliating)
   backs—covered by light grey hair with black spots
   voices—brayed like donkeys
   faces—grew long as muzzles

CHAPTER 33
1. By promises and flattery he collected all the children who did not like their books, carried them to Playland, let them play until they became donkeys and then took them to market and sold them, thus becoming a millionaire.
2. He didn't like either, but hay was better than straw.

CHAPTER 34
1. A live puppet, wriggling like an eel.
2. By telling him he would tell him his story.
3. He told him how he had almost become a real boy but he listened to evil companions and found himself a donkey.
4. The shark/dogfish swallowed him.

CHAPTER 35
2. We must find a way to escape immediately.

CHAPTER 36
1. The Tunny saved them.
2. He gave him a kiss.
3. He had pity on them after reminding Pinocchio that he had chased him away and hit him with a hammer.
4. He found him as a donkey in the gardener's barn.
5. He gave the snail money to save the fairy.
6. Because of his good heart that had changed to one that loved his parent and helped the poor.
7. Children who were naughty become good.